# DOG *Palaces*

By Brian Coleman

Photographs by Dan Mayers

Gibbs Smith, Publisher

TO ENRICH AND INSPIRE HUMANKIND

Salt Lake City | Charleston | Santa Fe | Santa Barbara

First Edition
10 09 08 07      5 4 3 2 1

Text © 2007 Brian Coleman
Photographs © 2007 Dan Mayers except
        cover and pages 73–75 © 2007 Gibbs Smith, Publisher
        page 62 © 2007 William Wright

Published by
Gibbs Smith, Publisher
P.O. Box 667
Layton, Utah 84041

Orders: 1.800.835.4993
www.gibbs-smith.com

Designed by Gabriella Hunter
Printed and bound in China

Library of Congress Cataloging-in-Publication Data

Coleman, Brian D.
    Dog palaces  : designer beds for pampered pooches / Brian Coleman ; photographs by Dan Mayers. — 1st ed.
        p. cm.
    ISBN 13: 978-1-4236-0023-7
    ISBN 10: 1-4236-0023-1
    1.  Dogs—United States. 2.  Pets—Housing—United States. 3.  Beds—United
States—Design and construction.  I. Title.

SF426.2.C66 2007
636.7'0831--dc22

*Acknowledgments*

·  ·  ·  ❧  ·  ·  ·

The author and photographer would like to thank all
the dogs, their owners and the designers that have
made this work possible. Brian wishes to thank his dog
Nanette for the many hours in his lap while he was
writing this book, and R.S. for his support and
encouragement. Dan wishes to also thank Lola and
Shilow, his two dogs, for all that they have taught and
shown him about loyalty and love.

# Contents

. . . ❧ . . .

# Preface

· · · · ❖ · · · ·

*If you can . . . (Anonymous)*

> *. . . start each day without caffeine, ready to greet the world,*
> *. . . get going without pep pills,*
> *. . . always be cheerful, ignoring aches & pains,*
> *. . . resist complaining & boring people with your troubles,*
> *. . . eat the same food everyday & be grateful for it,*
> *. . . understand when your loved ones are too busy to give you any time,*
> *. . . overlook it when those you love take it out on you when, through no fault of yours, something is wrong,*
> *. . . take criticism & blame without resentment,*
> *. . . ignore a friend's limited education & never correct him,*
> *. . . resist treating a rich friend better than a poor friend,*
> *. . . face the world without lies & deceit,*
> *. . . conquer tension without medical help,*
> *. . . relax without liquor,*
> *. . . sleep without the aid of drugs,*
> *. . . say that, deep in your heart, you have no prejudice of any kind,*

*Then, my friend, you are almost as good as your dog!*

Whether it's a petite palace á la Marie Antoinette, a modernistic glass house inspired by Philip Johnson, or a deluxe doggie-size travel trailer for that special vagabond with four legs and a tail, people's love for their dogs can best be seen in the homes they have created for their best friends. We traveled across the country from Manhattan to San Francisco searching for the very finest and most interesting palaces for dogs, homes that have been made with love and devotion—the very qualities that make dogs so special to their owners. This book will provide ideas and inspiration for dog owners everywhere to pamper their pets with a very special place of their own.

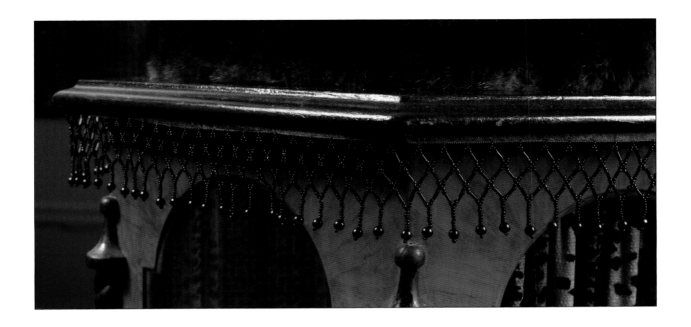

## Introduction

. . . ❖ . . .

"Dogs are man's best friends"—we've all heard the phrase. Just where did it come from? Attributed to Senator George Graham Vest of Missouri, "Dogs are man's best friends" was first used in 1870 in a famous speech he made in the case of *Burden v. Hornsby*. "Old Drum" had been the favorite dog of Charles Burden and was fatally shot by his neighbor, Leonidas Hornsby, when the unsuspecting pet wandered onto his property. Burden was enraged and sued Hornsby. The case eventually reached the Missouri Supreme Court and, much to the delight of dog lovers everywhere, Burden was awarded $50 in damages. (The local Chamber of Commerce even erected a statue of "Old Drum" on the lawn of the Johnson County Courthouse to honor the now-infamous mutt.) And ever since then Senator Vest's phrase has stuck as the most apt and succinct description that has been coined of the bond between people and their dogs.

# A COUNTRY CASTLE

## *in New Jersey*

· · · · ❖ · · ·

Phillis, an eleven-year-old Irish-bred Jack Russell terrier has been a fixture for more than a decade at Cottage Treasures, the antiques shop of Paul Dorman and John Frederich in Longvalley, New Jersey. Befitting her matronly status and years of raising many puppies, Phillis now prefers to spend most of her days in quiet repose. She still enjoys greeting customers, however, as they come into the shop, so Paul and John designed a simple but elegant bed for her to inhabit. An antique painted Asian cupboard, circa 1780, was converted into a bed by removing the shelves and installing vintage English chintz on the walls and bottom for a comfortable and stylish retreat. Lighting was unobtrusively installed in the ceiling of the cupboard for a more dramatic effect. The costly antique cabinet's value was not affected, as none of the changes were permanent. When Phillis is accompanying Paul and John on buying trips or at antiques shows, the doors of her castle are simply shut, and the cabinet remains a handsome piece of furniture in the shop. ❖

**Right:** *Phillis enjoys reposing in this antique Asian cupboard, which has been converted into an elegant bed for her.*

# CASUAL ELEGANCE

*in Buck's County, Pennsylvania*

. . . ❖ . . .

Richard and Linda Delier run a successful design business, The Interior Shop in bucolic Buck's County, Pennsylvania. Set amongst forests and rolling pastures, their home is a casual yet comfortable retreat, home to their two Yorkies and an Old English sheepdog. All of the dogs divide their time between home and the shop, where they delight in greeting customers and old friends. The Deliers have a collection of beds that their dogs enjoy and that can be used in both settings. Zachary-Arthur, their five-year-old Yorkie, is partial to lounging on his Oscar de la Renta "Norwich" bed. Developed by Mr. de la Renta and his wife, Annette, from beds they have created for their dogs on their Punta Cana estate, it is crafted in "dogwood" (distressed mahogany), and the frame features diamond and X motifs in a nod to the Orient. The perfect place, Zach can attest, to curl up for a long, dreamy nap.

Sometimes Zachary-Arthur and his companion, Ann-Marie, enjoy cuddling at night in their canopy bed from Ann Gish, Inc. Fabricated from stainless steel, the bed is a wonderful complement to their masters' bed. Pet-friendly, the fabrics are completely washable. Curtains and bedding are all Ann Gish silks and are accented by an assortment of throw pillows—the perfect lounging accents for a comfortable night's sleep.

**Above**: *Zachary-Arthur regally reclines on his Oscar de la Renta "Norwich" bed.* **Opposite**: *Ann Gish silks and throw pillows make the bed an inviting retreat.*

**Right:** *Zachary-Arthur and Ann-Marie enjoy lounging in their four-poster bed from Ann Gish.*

**Above:** *Hannah enjoys a moment's repose on her elegant art deco divan by Jeffco.* **Opposite:** *The gold frame is accented with a striking "Scaparelli" pink silk from Scalamandré, the color chosen to accent Hannah's markings.*

Hannah, the Deliers' Old English sheepdog, is the newest addition to the family and is admittedly a little spoiled. Hannah likes to spend her days greeting customers in the shop, and her friendly and ebullient nature makes her a natural. Her breed instinct is to herd sheep and protect them from wolves, and this comes in handy at times, especially when one client brings her small twins into the shop—Hannah becomes the perfect babysitter. Thus it's little surprise that the Deliers pulled out all the stops for Hannah's bed. Made by Jeffco, her "Chez Moi" art deco recamier is a reproduction of one originally owned by Helena Rubenstein and is finished in an exquisite gold crackle. The Deliers had the bed upholstered in Scalamandré's "Shangri-La" silk in a striking "Scaparelli" pink, which is the perfect highlight for Hannah's light gray, black, and white markings. While Hannah is usually too busy to spend long periods of time sleeping, she does admittedly enjoy an occasional snooze on her elegant divan.

**Above:** *The bed's intricate painting and gilding is highlighted with a black lacquer finish.*

**Above:** *Maxwell poses outside his favorite chinoiserie Louis Quinze bed.*

James Gill, Vice President of Design for the Interior Shop, is the proud father of Maxwell, a long-haired miniature dachshund who accompanies him to work several times a week. While he has a choice of beds, his favorite is his Louis Quinze floral-painted, gilt, black lacquer chinoiserie model with a serpentine dome top capped by a bronze finial. A suitably elegant bed for the dachshund who can often be found carrying a stick with his dachshund companion, Samuel. ❖

# A PUG PAVILION

## for a San Francisco Penthouse

. . . ❖ . .

When the owners of Mugsy Mugelsworth and Che Cheruba, two very well loved and admittedly very spoiled pugs, asked designers Daniel Krivens and Gary Nichols of Pollack Design to make a special bed for them, the designers knew just what was needed: something unique and unusual that would reflect the Moorish-style penthouse where Mugsy and Che lived but could also be practical and function as a piece of furniture. A glass-topped coffee table was created, its arabesque shape echoing the lines of the penthouse's architecture. The clear top allows visual access to the pugs reclining on their pillows as their owners sip cocktails or watch the fireplace on a foggy San Francisco evening. Both Mugsy and Che accompany their owners everywhere and enjoy being dressed in Chinese silk (actually children's outfits found in Chinatown) for those special events that require a touch more wit and panache, qualities at which these little emperors are adept. ❖

**Right:** *Mugsy and Che ham it up on their specially designed Pug Pavilion. The shape of the bed mimics the Moorish architecture of the pugs' penthouse.*

# HOTEL PAW-LOMAR

### *in San Francisco*

· · · · ✤ · · ·

Kimpton's Hotel Palomar, a popular resort based on the concept of "art in motion," is stylish and elegant but not elitist. Architect Andrew Alford designed a canine version of the artful urban retreat. The Hotel Paw-lomar is designed to give its four-legged visitors that same feeling of chic but comfortable sophistication. Colors were selected to be rich and seductive, and original artwork was incorporated in the bed, reflecting Kimpton's belief that art enriches all of our lives, regardless of what species we happen to be. Here Wrigley, a Polish sheepdog, shows that even with his bubbly personality he can still find time to relax and enjoy the finer aspects of life. ✤

# BAUHAUS BASICS

*in San Francisco*

. . . . . ❖ . . . .

Bauhaus was designed by the Beeline Group for the five small dogs of Lynne Tingle, the founder of The Milo Foundation Animal Rescue. Built around a hexagon-shaped room with three entrances, the structure is a place where the dogs can sleep, play or even use as a racetrack. One corner is an in-cove lined with stainless steel, designed as a spot for the dogs to wet their whistles. The back panel is an acrylic door that opens easily for cleaning. Two rubber-mat-covered ramps lead to the second level, which is usually claimed by Lynne's elderly Chihuahua, Queen What's What, as her vantage point. A removable ramp leads from the ground floor to the third-floor balcony. The top level accommodates the human factor, and thus a stainless steel and acrylic countertop bar with a snack drawer was made so that Lynne and her friends can relax, have a cocktail, and watch their little cherubs frolic after a hard day's work. Here, Maggie happily models the bed, showing its splendor. ❖

**Right:** *Made for both humans and their canines, the Bauhaus Basic has several levels with connecting ramps for the frolicking dogs. Humans can have a drink and sit around this combination bar and dog house.*

# LAPS *of* LUXURY

## *in New York City*

·  ·  ·  ❖  ·  ·  ·

New York designer Christopher Matson acquired his miniature Chihuahua, Lady Bug, in 2001, and the tiny bundle of charm quickly became his constant companion. Nestled into his suit pocket, the young Lady Bug went along to meetings with clients, and it wasn't long before she was a favorite at galleries and showrooms around the city. Now that she has reached her full adult stature of three pounds, Lady Bug has become a bit too large for suit pockets, so Christopher has constructed her a proper residence of her own.

Lady Bug enjoys playing host to her stuffed animal friends at her conservative, antique neoclassical pavilion. Christopher sensitively restored the bed, found in a Connecticut antiques shop, by painting it in Farrow & Ball's "Cord" and lightly overglazing in umber. Inspired by Palladian architecture and traditional designs, the classic lines of the bed were finished in plaster gesso and gold leaf.

Lady Bug likes dressing for the occasion and is seen on the following page in her award-winning gown constructed with fabrics from Dedar. (The costume won first prize in the 2005 New York Canine Couture Contest, benefitting the New York Humane Society.) Constructed of an ivory silk moiré with black-flocked velvet, the dress evokes an Elizabethan elegance. The ostrich plume collar is trimmed with black sequins and satin rosettes with a vintage rhinestone clasp.

An exotic pavilion was also designed as an Ottoman harem befitting an odalisque such as Lady Bug. The exterior is finished in mink and leopard and trimmed with black Bohemian crystals for a luxurious and regal look. The domed top easily lifts off to reveal a sparkling, gilded interior (and makes for easy off-season toy storage and cleaning). Whether her fancy is that of an exotic canine princess or a more proper matron with impeccable manners, Lady Bug now has her own appropriate laps of luxury. ❖

**Right:** *Lady Bug likes to dress fashionably in her silk moiré skirt and ostrich plume collar.*

**Above:** *An Ottoman palace finished in mink and leopard and trimmed with black crystals is perfect for Lady Bug's exotic moods.* **Opposite:** *Detail of the Ottoman palace shows beautiful attention to detail.*

# THE SAN FRANCISCO

## Pet "Nd" Table

. . . ✤ . . .

The Huntsman Architectural Group designed this "Nd" table and doghouse for multiuse of parent and dog. Built on castors, the table can be easily wheeled from the living room to the bedroom. Here Yorkie Maggie models the comfort and convenience of the Pet Nd Table with its simple yet elegant design. ✤

# DOG BITES BED

## *in the Bay Area*

· · · ❖ · · ·

It would seem that a dog wants for nothing save a good walk, a rigorous scratch, a nap, and of course, a big, juicy steak. However, that steak is always just out of reach, especially if the dog is a little guy and can't reach the countertop. What better way to indulge a bit than to give your dog that one object of desire, at least in spirit? Here, a dog bed is formed in the shape of a large steak, complete with a soft built-in mattress and a water bowl set flush in the surface. Marty, an energetic greyhound, loves the simplicity of this bed, a place where he can happily flop, exhausted but content, after a round of vigorous races around his master's ankles. Designed by Sasaki Associates has combined creativity and problem solving to provide exceptional interior design services for more than fifty years. ❖

# CAMPING

## in Canada

. . . . ❖ . . .

Judson Beaumont is a talented artist in Vancouver, British Columbia, who appreciates the need to include our four-legged friends in our lives, whether we are at home or traveling. Judson has designed a miniature camper trailer for that special pet. Made entirely of fiberglass, the camper is highly detailed, down to diminutive rivets and wheels that really turn. The Pet Camper comes with two trays for food and a laminate interior for easy cleaning. Here Puffy, a sweet-tempered shih tzu, takes a break from her favorite meal, arroz con pollo, in her camper. Judson designs one-of-a-kind furniture and art across North America. ❖

Beautiful British Columbia
GRRRRR

**Left:** *Puffy can relax in style with her miniature travel camper made entirely of fiberglass.*

# A THRONE FOR A

## *Manhattan Princess*

. . . ❖ . . .

It's no secret that New Yorkers love to spoil their pets, and one of their favorite shops is Larry Roth's Precious Pets on Manhattan's Upper East Side. Here, canines are treated like royalty at the day care center while their owners shop for suitable accessories. Bella, admittedly a pampered one-year-old pug, was instantly attracted to this Star of India bed. Constructed of sturdy anodized bronze in a blackened patina with an open canopy, the bed is graced with multicolored jeweled Austrian crystals and topped with a crown; it even comes with matching food bowls.

Bella is quite partial to jewels and, in fact, comes to her day care each morning sporting a different piece of jewelry, much to the envy of both her canine and human friends. The bed, all agree, was the perfect throne for this little Manhattan princess. ❖

**Above:** *The Star of India bed has a matching feeding station.*

**Above:** *A jeweled crown tops the regally designed bed.*

Other visitors to Precious Pets prefer a more relaxed look befitting the spa setting. A favorite bed is the blue-and-white striped cabana from Italy. The soft cotton awning is also available in red and white. Molly, a longhaired Chihuahua, gets ready for her day of relaxation. ✤

**Left:** *Whether it's a day at the beach or at the spa, the cabana bed from Italy is perfect for this diminutive Chihuahua.*

# VICTORIAN SPLENDOR

*in San Francisco*

. . . ❖ . . .

San Francisco is best known for its exuberant and whimsical Victorian homes, and so Huntsman Architectural Group appropriately incorporated this iconographic style in their updated version of a classic Queen Anne, this one for man's best friend. Traditional detailing includes arches, turrets, and a steeply gabled roof constructed in utilitarian materials such as plywood. An exterior shell of clear Plexiglas and wood trim painted in a confection of colors reminiscent of local Victorian homes was added to allow a view of the interior structure and reinforce the idea that the trim is simply an appliqué. When Coco and Bella, Italian greyhounds, were introduced to their new home, it was an instant match. Coco, the older and more mature of the two (she loves having her nails filed!), immediately curled up inside for a quick nap. Bella, younger and more energetic, found her new home a perfect spot to store her stuffed toys and has been known to hide her treats there as well, trying to eat them on the sly when her companion isn't looking. ❖

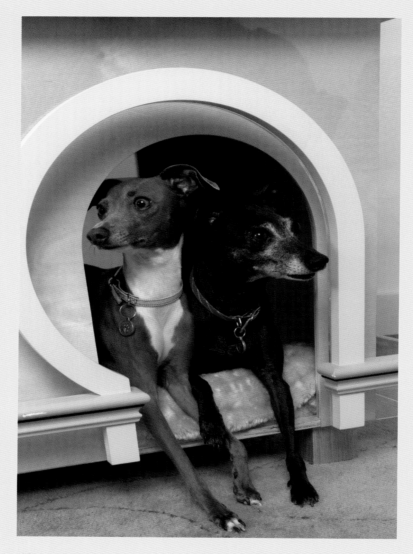

**Above:** *Bella and Coco share their house amicably.* **Opposite:** *Queen Anne architecture is appliquéd onto the Plexiglas frame for an update on the San Francisco classic, this time for canines.*

# SUTTON PLACE

*Classic Design*

· · · · ✤ · · ·

Sutton Place is one of New York's more desirable addresses. Large prewar apartments overlook the Hudson River and hearken back to the days of luxury and sophisticated living for which New York is so famous. Emma Jane Pilkington, a New York designer, has elegantly restored her own Sutton Place apartment with classic works of art and judiciously chosen antiques. When she came across the circa-1810 French pine doll bed tucked away in the attic of an antiques store, she fell in love with its mellow patina and instantly thought of her fawn pug Bizmark. When he is not cuddling, Bizmark is partial to frequent naps and really needs a proper bed of his own. Emma had a down mattress constructed for the bed and covered it in a Christopher Hyland silk velvet sporting fanciful, mythical animals. A silk velvet cushion at the head of the bed in a lively leopard print from Clarence House was the perfect elegant accent. The simple, rustic tonality of the bed contrasts handsomely against the elegant marquetry of the apartment's painted floors, creating a sweet folly for both Bizmark and his mistress to enjoy. ✤

**Right**: *Bizmark loves luxury, especially the silk velvet cushions on his bed.*

# MODERNISM
# IN SAN FRANCISCO

*The Bark House*

·  ·  ·  ❖  ·  ·  ·

Philip Johnson is one of the masters of modern architecture and his famous "Glass House" in New Canaan, Connecticut, remains an icon of design. Susan LaBlanc's Bark House was inspired by Johnson's masterpiece and is intended for the discriminating dog—one who understands that he is superior to his owner in style and taste. Only such a dog could appreciate the piece for what it really is: perfection simplified. The transparent walls allow the residents to observe their surroundings, and nature is reflected in the tree trunks and etched on the glass walls. Made entirely of locally harvested materials, Bark House does not offgas, thus protecting the pet's health. Here, Mugsy models the home for us, coyly popping out of the central trunk. ❖

*Right: A modern dog such as Mugsy appreciates Bark House's reference to Philip Johnson's famous Glass House design.*

# A PASSEMENTERIE PALACE

## *for a Grande Dame in Seattle*

. . . ❖ . . .

Nanette, a twelve-year-old Yorkie, is the grande dame of her Seattle household. It is thus only befitting a lady in her station of life that she resides in an appropriate residence. Designer Eric Jensen has created a palace for her with the very best of Scalamandré passementerie. Based on the traditions of the grand, traveling tents of royalty, silk trim, tassels, and cording were chosen and no expense was spared. A six-inch molded wooden base was used as the foundation and a handcarved stair entry ramp covered in blue-and-white leopard stripe set the stage for Nanette's grand entrances. Sumptuous green-and-gold-striped silk curtains were lined in yellow silk for a dream-filled slumber. A ruched sky-blue taffeta crown was added and trimmed with handmade mold fringes and a coral rosette with a multicolored loop fringe stamen was added at the center. Jewel-toned tassels and gimps were used on all of the leading edges for an opulent look. The crowning touch, 24-karat gilded flag finials and spires make this a bed that always beckons with fanfare. ❖

# DELSEA'S TOOLBOX

*in San Francisco*

. . . ❖ . . .

Designed by Gensler, a global architecture and design firm, Delsea's Toolbox is designed to support the active lifestyle of a dog on the go. The habitat combines style and substance, exhibited by the glamour of a boudoir along with the practicality of a toolbox—befitting the dog of a general contractor. Drawers hold everything from jewelry and leashes to toys and snacks and make it easy for Dad to take his dog along with him to job sites. Bailey, a Welsh terrier, models the Toolbox, showing that it is a comfortable home for any small- to medium-size dog. ❖

# PETOIA LOUNGE

*in San Francisco*

. . . ❧ . . .

Knoll has been a leader in design since its founding in 1938, and the distinctive seating of Harry Bertoia has been part of its line since 1952. Simple industrial wire rods have been made into design icons of machine-age furniture by Bertoia. This elegant pet lounge is made to order, sized especially for your pet. Upholstered in Knoll Textiles "Cuddle Cloth," it is irresistible for not only pets but appreciative humans as well, and so Knoll wisely includes an owner's chair with a matching seat pad. Here, well-mannered Maggie models the chair, displaying her innate sense of fashion and style. ❧

# ORIENTAL CHARM

*in the East Village*

· · · ❖ · · ·

Laura Lobdell, a talented artist who makes her home in New York City's vibrant East Village, shares her apartment with Xiao, a pampered Japanese Chin. After reading *The Art of Raising a Puppy* by the Monks of New Skete, she realized that Xiao was a den animal that needed a private environment of his own. Laura discovered the beauty of Marie Antoinette's eighteenth-century doghouses on a trip to Paris, and, as the Japanese Chin originated in the Imperial Court of China, it seemed only natural to make him a pavilion of his own in a fanciful chino:serie design. Laura constructed a trompe l'oeil tent top crowned with an ostrich plume. On the interior, she painted shelves of Chinese porcelain vases and traditional Chinese lattice-screened windows looking out to a garden. In one side window, she painted a bird in a birdcage to keep Xiao company, while glowing paper lanterns "hang" in the other. The interior floor was gilded and overlaid with hand-painted Asian blossoms. The ceiling, from which a jade chandelier hangs, was silver-leafed to evoke an evening sky. Chinese silk brocade curtains trimmed in silk Houles pom-poms were chosen to frame the front of the house, and a pair of Foo dogs guard the entrance.

Xiao loves his personal pagoda and is content to nap away the afternoon on his fluffy, quilted silk pillow and miniature cashmere and silk throws. ❖

**Above:** *Foo dogs guard the entrance to this regal dog palace.* **Opposite:** *Hand-painted details include trompe l'oeil shelves of Oriental vases.*

# VILLA CHIHUAHUA

*in San Francisco*

. . . ❖ . . .

Architects John C. Barone and Jason P. Langkammerer, principals of At-Six Architecture, were inspired by Le Corbusier's classic gem of modern design, the Villa Savoye, to create this smaller-scale interpretation for their diminutive two-year old Chihuahua, Diego. With big blue-green eyes and a personality that belies his tiny stature, Diego charms everyone he meets.

A covered, slightly raised, cavelike sleeping sanctuary on the lower level is connected by a ramp to the upper living level, which is raised on pilots and furnished with a pouf for causal lounging and is even fitted with an aqua refresher. Diego appreciates his "machine for modern living" and particularly enjoys its protection from clumsy human feet. When atop its upper level, he stands proudly, as tall as a terrier or one of those other, silly, larger dogs. ❖

# YEAR OF THE DOG

*in San Francisco*

·   ·   ·   ✤   ·   ·   ·

When the TSAO Design Group of San Francisco made their Take Time Out pet palace, it was with a specific goal of celebrating the 2006 Chinese Lunar New Year's Year of the Dog. Cleverly designed and fabricated, it was made as the perfect place for a furry friend to take time out. The lacquer finish is safe, durable, and washable, and the interior is lined with a warm, soft, removable carpet, a comfy spot for a snooze. Maggie, a four-year-old Yorkie, loves to chase squirrels and pigeons in the park or run on the beach with her best friend, a black lab. When she is worn out she snuggles in her bed, glad to take a nap, often with her favorite stuffed monkey. ✤

# UPPER EAST SIDE ELEGANCE

*in New York City*

· · · ❖ · · ·

It was a cold and rainy night when New York designer Betsy Boggs noticed an injured dog stranded in the center of a busy highway. Without regard for her own safety, she dashed across the traffic and rescued the hapless, homeless creature. Betsy named the mixed breed papillon and King Charles spaniel Precious, to reflect her special fortune. Precious proved to be a loving and devoted companion and inspired Betsy to design a bed befitting her regal nature. Based on the ornate dog palaces that Marie Antoinette had built for her six papillons at Versailles (one of whom she carried to the guillotine when she was beheaded in 1793; the dog was, fortunately, spared), Betsy constructed a palace fit for any canine royalty. Made of handcrafted rich walnut and upholstered in traditional coral silk velvet with gold leaf and burnished trim, the Marie Antoinette palace has a warm, modern opulence. While Precious only lived another four years before succumbing to a preexisting illness, her bed was so popular with both her canine and human friends that Betsy decided to design a complete line of custom pet palaces in honor of Precious, based on the best of traditional design. Here, Daisy, a longhaired Chihuahua, models the Marie Antoinette model.

**Above:** *Gold leaf and burnished trim highlight the bed's expert craftsmanship.*
**Previous:** *Fashioned after the royal dog residences at Versailles, the Marie Antoinette Pet Palace is finely crafted with gilded walnut and upholstered in coral silk velvet—certainly fit for any canine royalty.*

**Above**: *The Ottoman Precious Palace is a favorite retreat for Elizabeth, a Chihuahua with an attitude that belies her tiny stature; the bed also doubles as an ottoman with extra seating.*

The Ottoman Precious Palace was designed as an amusing and updated take on the traditions of the Turkish court. Shown here in black faux leather with pewter biker studs and chain, a spiked collar, and an ultra-suede zebra cushion, it is not only home for Elizabeth, a tiny but fierce miniature Chihuahua with an attitude, but also doubles as extra seating for guests.

**Above:** *Gilded wooden bells decorate the corners of the canopy.* **Opposite:** *Sugar loves holding court in her Chinese pagoda. The double-tiered pagoda is upholstered in rich gold and red silk from Quadrille.*

Betsy looked throughout the world for inspiration and produced the Precious Pagoda Palace, based on the exotic traditions of Southeast Asia and the Orient. Constructed in wood, the two-tiered pagoda is lacquered in a rich raspberry red and upholstered in "Quadrille," an opulent gold, green and red brocade; the tented corners are accented with golden wood bells. All the cushions are removable and easily dry-cleaned for ease of maintenance. Here Sugar, a spoiled but loving Maltese, rests in her lap of luxury, holding court while her favorite humans attend to her every need.

The four-poster Louis XVI Precious Palace was inspired by the classic design of the French court. Shown here in yellow and blue silk brocade with coordinating French blue silk trim and linings, the curtains and skirt are removable for dry cleaning. The woodwork, including the Louis XVI legs, has been glazed in ivory. Daisy, a longhaired Chihuahua, enjoys reclining amongst the curtains when she seeks a moment of respite from her busy day.

**Left:** *Daisy reclines among the yellow-and blue-brocade cushions of the Louis XIV Precious Palace, inspired by the opulent design of the French court. Silk trim and linings complement the brocade draperies.*

**Above**: *Upholstered in Moroccan silk paisley, the tent is accented with red glass beads and an ostrich plume on top.* **Opposite**: *The Mongolian Tent Precious Palace is the perfect headquarters for the general of the household. Here, Bomber surveys his ranks.*

The stylish Mongolian Tent Precious Palace was inspired by those used by Genghis Khan and his officers in their campaigns. The walls are upholstered in an opulent red and cream Moroccan silk paisley, and the bed is crowned with a gold finial and the ultimate military accent—an ostrich plume—to designate high rank and royalty. Here, Bomber, an admittedly bossy Maltese, surveys his ranks from his campaign headquarters.

**Opposite:** *The USS Precious is both a footstool and a home for the crew of this household, and it's obvious that Max the red Persian is at the helm.* **Above:** *Upholstered in marine-blue ultra suede, the bed is trimmed in white cotton rope and accented with brass detailing.*

The whimsical USS Precious functions as both a charming nautical palace and a footstool for the captain of the home. Shown here in plush marine-blue English ultra suede, it has white cotton rope trim and brass finishing details. Of course, when there are cats to consider, one should think twice about who is truly in charge, as Max the resident red Persian makes abundantly clear to her fellow shipmate Maggie, a Maltese who has become resigned to her station in life. ✤

# HUMANE TREATMENT TESTAMENT

## *in San Francisco*

. . . ❖ . . .

When San Francisco passed Pet Ordinance number 41.12 in 2005, it ensured the humane treatment of dogs, making it illegal to leave them unattended without water, shelter, proper confinement, and other important safeguards. Gensler, a global architecture and design firm, celebrated this ordinance with this bed—or is it art, a piece of furniture, or a legal document? Most likely all of the above, attests its owner, Michael Cunningham, whose two miniature dachshunds, Zeke and Hank, enjoy supporting the rights of their fellow canines in an admittedly stylish manner. Michael owns the popular San Francisco pet store Babies, where Zeke and Hank are frequently in residence. ❖

**Right**: *The pet ordinance is printed on the sides of the bed and becomes a piece of art in its own right as well as a legal document.*

**Above:** *Zeke loves to retreat to the comfortable tent by Wagwear and hide his bones inside.*

**Above:** *Hank and Zeke enjoy a peaceful moment together in their Wagwear tent.*

On the odd days the boys are left at home, they often retreat to their Wagwear Tee Pee Hound Lounge, the perfect place for an afternoon nap. And since their parents never look inside, it's a perfect spot for hiding toys and treats. ❖

# DOGGOU:
# THE NEW YEAR OF THE DOG

*San Francisco Style*

. . . ❖ . . .

MBH, an established architectural firm, combined their creative efforts to make a pet habitat that reflects the Bay Area's ethnic roots. In celebration of the Chinese New Year of the Dog (2006), the "Doggou" is a modern fusion of traditional Chinese cabinetry platform and canopy beds designed for a small or medium dog (*gou* in Chinese). The Doggou was designed as a versatile space with two interlocking volumes that serve multiple needs, from storage and feeding to just plain comfort and style. Constructed of a series of sliding drawers and a central living enclosure with a top storage compartment, the sleek, dark coffee–stained bamboo plywood is punctuated with Chinese characters and contrasted with richly colored textured cushions in the interior. The Doggou is an elegant ensemble, a functional form that creates a harmonious flow of energy for all to enjoy. Here Bailey, a culturally sensitive Welsh terrier, shows that this dynamic creation can be enjoyed by everyone. ❖

**Right**: *Soft, furry cushions add color and comfort to the interior.*

**Previous**: *Traditional Chinese cabinetry is fused with creative canine design to celebrate the Year of the Dog (gou in Chinese).*

# Sources for Beds

· · · ❧ · · ·

# Paws for Reflection

· · · ❧ · · ·

Many of the beds featured in this book were courtesy of Pets Are Wonderful Support PAWS, San Francisco.

PAWS is a volunteer-based organization that provides for the comprehensive needs of companion animals for low-income persons with HIV/AIDS and other disabling illnesses. By providing these essential support services, educating the larger community on the benefits of the human-animal bond, and advocating for the rights of disabled individuals to keep service animals, PAWS improves the health and well-being of both animals and people.

PAWS holds an annual fund raiser called Petchitecture, for which pet habitats are custom built by architects and furniture designers. The pieces featured in this book represent some of those creations. For more information on PAWS, please visit their Website at www.pawssf.org.